ALMOST TOMORROW

To Judy
Tks for Talking w/me
at Food & Button.
Jos,
Ray Nargis

The Poems of
Ray Nargis

Raven Productions, Inc
Ely, Minnesota

Text © 2008 by Ray Nargis

Published 2008 by Raven Productions, Inc
P.O. Box 188, Ely, MN 55731
(218) 365-3375   www.ravenwords.com

Printed in Minnesota
United States of America
10 9 8 7 6 5 4 3 2 1

Cover photo and author photo © Steve Foss Images

Library of Congress Cataloging-in-Publication Data

Nargis, Ray, 1952-
  Almost tomorrow : the poetry of Ray Nargis.
     p. cm.
  ISBN 978-0-9794202-7-6 (pbk.)
  I. Title.
  PS3614.A695A79 2007
  811'.6--dc22
                                    2007033926

To my sons, who believed
long after the time passed
when they should have.

TABLE OF CONTENTS

When I was a child I dreamt I could fly.
Not your run-of-the-mill flying dream
Where you wake up just before you fall off the cliff
And snap your neck
And all the covers are strewn and you're breathing so hard
Your partner says:
"What the hell is wrong with you? You kicked me!"
No, I had a flying dream unlike any others I have ever known.
In my dream
I'm a foot off the ground and moving in slow motion.
Like a balloon following after a kid. Like I've escaped gravity.
Like I'm in a movie and someone comes up to me and says:
"I see you're flying there, what's that about then?"

Or maybe the dream where you're on your bike
At the top of a long hill and it's that perfect fall day,
Not even a day, the perfect fall moment
And there is no wind, no other people, no sound.
And it has just rained a little
But now the sun comes out and you push off
And never pedal once, just glide and glide,
Dips and swells and hairpin turns and the leaves start to drop
And it goes on and on. Past farmlands and through little villages,
Over wooden covered bridges,
The kind they don't even build anymore.
And the ride takes on a life of its own,
Like a soloist in the orchestra,
And you try to sustain it for as long as you can.
And it becomes mythic and you disappear into myth
Because it's your dream and you can.

They say that Yogis and seventh-degree Tao masters can levitate.
And why not?
Science tells us we use only ten percent of our brains,
And most politicians only half of that.

They say our bodies are made of the same stuff as the stars,
Which makes sense
Because if we all want to go to heaven
We have to pass that way anyhow.
I had a writer friend who said: "When I die,
I'm going to a better place.
And if I don't like it there, I'm moving on."
I'd like to think he's out there right now
Prowling around the back streets of heaven,
Looking for a tin of chewing tobacco
And hobnobbing with the famous and the dead.

And then there is another kind of flying dream,
The kind where you're stuck in a life you weren't put here to have.
And everyone around you says:
"No, you're just an ugly duckling, not a swan."
But it's as if you can just see it out there sometimes,
This other you.
And so you burn your whole life to the ground,
You tear the world in two pieces
And toss the halves into the void,
You walk out of the house one night for milk and eggs
And you never come back. And maybe you find what you need
And maybe you don't and maybe it changes over time
And becomes less of a compulsion and obsession.
And it doesn't matter because you had a little life
And you went looking for a larger one.

Because you had a dream once,
So dim now you can hardly remember it.
And in that dream, in that dream, you flew.

There is a place I go sometimes so sad and lonely.
It takes about a week to get there and it is as if,
With the very first step, the road slants downhill,
Gravity conspires, the incubus and succubus push and pull
And the moon eclipses reason and hope every moment.

There are others on this same road.
I can see their dim forms in the half-light,
But I can't help them; I can only watch them disappear
Like an ancient sailing vessel's mast dissolves on the horizon.
Even if I only wave or nod, they scurry into the night
Terrified of the beast they imagine in my form.
Sometimes I hear them call out to me in a fitful night's sleep,
But the syntax is muted and I can't understand their message.

I have been lucky so far to always find my way back
From these night journeys, but who knows how long luck lasts,
And anyway, think of that word itself, "luck,"
A Greek colloquial expression, a nickname and blanket
For everything the ancients didn't understand, thus feared.

I once toured a former mental hospital.
In the hundred-year-old logbook were listed
"Causes for Confinement," a sobriquet for why
People had been locked up. On thousands of entries,
Mostly of women, read one word: "Melancholia,"
Which they once thought came from acid in the spleen
And treated with ice baths and incarceration.

Even though we never met, or may never meet,
My fellow travelers on the night road.
I know you all and you are not alone.
Perhaps it is only cold comfort I too offer,
But if on some winter's night you are driving
And you happen upon a bowed and ragged figure
At the edge of your headlights, a figure hooded and afraid,
That will be me and I am your brother.

CITIZEN'S ARREST

Even after he had quit his job as a lawman
They came to my father for advice.
Driving up the long crushed-stone driveway
On summer evenings
To accept glasses of iced tea
And sit in white lawn chairs in the sassafras grove.
Passing long-barreled Colts and Brownings
Back and forth.
Talking baseball or kids or truck parts.
Listening to whippoorwills
Or the exegesis of my old man
On some matter of local concern.

These were the men who carried guns.
Who had something on everyone.
Who directed traffic around accidents on the highway
And pistol-whipped surly drunks.
Cool blunt men who never questioned the laws
They doled out on rural roads
Or in crosstown taverns.
Tough customers with steady hands
And eyes for anything out of place.

One night I was sitting with my grandfather and dad
By the lake.
They drove up to the cottage
In a rush of siren and blue lights,
Told my father Old Man Foster had killed his wife
And was holed up in his shack down the road.
We piled into Grandpa Ed's black Chevrolet
And went to have a look-see.

In uniformed silence
They stood around dumbfounded
As the old drunk held them at bay with random gunshots.
My father in his Hawaiian shirt
And porkpie straw hat
Walked up the front steps and stood a few moments
Talking through the door
As the frogs in the bayou drowned out his whispers.

Fireflies had just begun to glint across the swamp
When the door opened
And a hand extending from the cool black interior
Came through the doorway empty.
My father took the hand and led Foster
Down the narrow path to the squad car.
Talking the whole time in low tones,
Nonchalantly slipping the gun
Out of the old man's other hand,
Petting his shoulder
And crooning long vowel sounds.
Calming him as one might a terrified animal.

THE DEVIL

Oh, he's had his moments, I'll give him that.
But mostly he's a loser, a piker, and a buffoon.
The Fallen Angel is more a pratfall artist.
More the least common denominator of any equation.
The lowest rung on the ladder that gives way.
He's a spilled milk and stolen lunch money kind of guy.
He's the motel clerk who registers the TV evangelist
And his mistress and then calls The National Enquirer.

The officious jerk at the party who sucks the air from the room,
Telling the same off-colored jokes year after year
And standing too close with bad breath.
The devil can't do much right, so does everything wrong.
Maybe he got beat up too much in grade school, or his dad
Was an overbearing braggart and bully
And the template just took.
He isn't fussy about the big picture,
Just messes with the stage props.
He's the one who invented the mail-in rebate,
The cancer-causing additive,
The half truth, the white lie, the bottom line and Reality TV.
He can't even play his trump card – Death – at the right time,
Laying it down too early or too late and losing the pot.

And he whines about Jesus and getting kicked out of heaven
And how Disease and Pestilence and Wrath
Are somebody else's fault.
Death is the black bird in the parking lot
Picking dead bugs out of the car's grill and burning his beak.
He's the half worm you find in the apple,
The newscaster who's all style and no substance,
Mouthing whatever anyone says in his earpiece
And moving on to the next story.
When he's bored he'll mismatch your socks, hijack an airbus,
Put *E.coli* in a bag of spinach,
Or give a C.E.O. another golden parachute, make you lose hope.

Your boss isn't the devil; he's an idiot all by himself.
Your mother-in-law isn't the devil;
She just wanted her daughter to have a better life,
But really, she wanted to have one herself.
The IRS isn't the devil; he just does their books.
The Neanderthal who did your root canal isn't the devil,
Although he might be.
I saw this movie once where a character said:
"The greatest trick the devil ever played
Was making us believe he didn't exist."
But that's not quite right either.
Because there is no devil.
He's just a rube and a rummy and a reprobate.
As for any real evil in this world,
Evil that isn't Fate or Fantasy or Happenstance,
I'm afraid we've got that one covered all by ourselves.

There is a point in sickness
Where you have done everything
And all you can do is sit in the rocking chair
At four in the morning
Covered in every blanket you own
And look out the window at the neighbor's border collie
Trying to herd snow devils in the street.
And then you just take it.
Endurance is a grey fog on the seashore
Hiding the view from the vacationers
Who paid a thousand bucks a day to come there.
Endurance is hauling boxes in some third world factory
So you can buy a pair of two-hundred-dollar jeans.
Endurance sucks, but so does gravity.
And sometimes putting in your time,
Breathing is all you have.

"In my youth I was intemperate in my habits
And irresponsible in my choice of friends."
Mr. Mark Twain wrote that line
And truer words were never spoken.
I always had a constitution
And physical fortitude to throw off sickness.
Health was an oyster slurped down
On the way through a magnum of wine
On a deserted beach with a beautiful woman
Under a full moon's smile.
Health was the given in every situation.
Now, after watching the rivers of my life
Run to the sea for over 50 years, the worm has turned.
Now, with fewer and fewer friends still marching around
Ready for any adventure,
Perhaps a more reasonable approach is advisable.

Many cannot adapt – the world is full,
Or should I say empty,
Of cases where genetic stubbornness led to eradication.
Where the undaunted became the Dodo Bird of values.
The stoic, The Snail Darter of ideals.
But so hard to set aside
The mantle of leadership of The Unconcerned.
The scepter of The Sanctimonious.
The crown jewels of The Carefree,
To take off the wolf's mask and cloak, and live as a sheep.
To linger and vacillate
Where once you bulled through any china shop.

They tell in every religion about the meek and mild,
About acceptance and forgiveness.
Stories of how the sun wins the bet with the wind,
About which can make the man take off his coat.
Tales about passing through the eye of a needle,
Which I'm not sure I'd do even for good health.
Stories of instruction and wisdom,
Of walking with kindness and grace
Throughout all the days of your life.
Perhaps it is time for some diplomacy
In my war with the world.
I know there is something to all of this
Because Confucius posed riddles that couldn't be solved
And Jesus spoke in parables – told stories –
Plus he was a carpenter and liked to fish.
In the sea of illness, do we not all walk on water?

Mark Twain once said, "I am not 'an' American,
I am 'the' American." He may have been right.
But now there are 300 million of us.
In the '60s there were 200 million,
And when I was a boy, not so many years ago,
They still brought milk and eggs down the street
With a horse-drawn wagon.
My hand to God on this, and it was not that long ago.
Obviously in the intervening 50 years people have been busy.
Busy having babies, importing babies,
Bringing babies across some sweltering border at night
To get their chance at The American Dream.
Obviously a Growth Industry.

And what is that dream?
The new Lexus will parallel park itself with motion sensors,
People inject animal fat into their lips,
Have eye surgery with lasers,
Run marathons on artificial legs, and 80 is the new 40.
A car costs what a house used to, a house what a company did.
"But our souls are not for sale," say both the Left and the Right.
Of course we still like our politicians like we like our coffee –
Rich and oily. But Will Rogers was right:
"We have the finest government money can buy."

Kit Carson killed as many Indians as he could find in the 1820s,
Then married one
And spent his last years bemoaning the Lost West.
Rush Limbaugh has admitted being addicted
To both prescription painkillers and Viagra,
And don't even get me started
On Nixon and his whole gang.
Obviously heroes are in short supply – just ask Barry Bonds.

What then are we to do with these 300 million Americans?

Where do we tell them to go to school
When crazy people walk in with guns?
Where to get a drink of water,
Walk down the street at night,
Eat food that hasn't been irradiated
Or filled with growth hormones?
Perhaps a country that cares more about
Bling Bling and the Bottom Line and Living Forever
Than its own kids
May need some constructive surgery.
And now they tell us we aren't even citizens anymore –
We're consumers.

The greatest poet in American history,
Walt Whitman, once wrote,
"I see great things in this America.
I see a universe of possibility."
Of course the press in Whitman's time called him
"A rogue, a scoundrel" and "a man of the people."

A DEAF LOVER

This day
I walked
Between those
Two bloodless birches
You called the "sisters of indecision"
And felt the warm tide repeat its warning:
We are more or less vagrants
Quarrelling within a length of
Skin, passing jauntily.

Your hands call my name.
Telling me your needs:
Come into my arms.
Turn your face back into a kiss.
Mix your legs with mine, your misalliance.
Your spit and garish yearnings.

The night we were introduced
I warned myself not to jab
And parry with you – truculent purveyor.
We spoke of hollyhocks.
Of the meaning of prayerful sleep.
Of suggested obsession.

We will never know enough.
Never be enough.
Never mount a grand enough offensive.
A fuse of vapor.
A cherished fashion.
Something reticent.

There is rattling in the self-conscious
Embryo of ethics.
A tic and palpitation of the unwanted child.
It pleads to tremble
In a caress of separate light.
It stalks every denial
And ruptures every parting,
Healed again only by something
Vague as reconciliation.

It is not the cat in the night
Or the discourteous callings of the audience.
Hissing was once popular at political events.
Now our politicians can't be touched by mere mortals.
Nor should most of them be.
To register dissatisfaction with something is no longer in vogue.
For now, if you protest anything, you're an enemy of the state.
Oddly enough, I thought we were the state.

There's an old saying when playing cards:
That if you look around the table
And can't tell who's the patsy, then you are the mark.
And aren't we all?
Robber barons still rape the whole world –
Check your conscience at the door
And go about the business of diversifying your portfolio.
But now the worst sins imaginable in our PC universe
Are to light up a cigarette indoors
Or to say something gender specific.

A doctor said to me not long ago
That he was tired of treating patients
Who wouldn't take care of themselves.
Think of the ego and hubris inherent in that statement,
Like a parent giving up
Teaching a child to walk after six weeks
Because the learning curve was too steep.
Like people trading marriage partners
Because they no longer fit their lifestyle.
And God forbid you should ever violate someone's personal space
Or make an ethnic joke.
And we've picked the most insipid person in the room
To run the whole deal.

They say the squeaky wheel gets the grease,
That every dog has his day,
That might makes right and the devil take the hindmost.
That if you give a man enough rope
He'll hang himself.
They say if you string enough cliches together
You'll come up with a universal truth.
Maybe the early bird does get the worm,
And the second mouse gets the cheese.

So perhaps if we spit into the wind enough times
We can convince ourselves it's raining.
And maybe the emperor really has no clothes
And pigs will fly someday, but I doubt it.
But then, I've been wrong before.

If you ripped the bloody heart out of any man's chest
A part of what you'd find would be wolf heart.
So it has been written and so believed.
In the iconography of America
Nothing stands up to the timber wolf.
And it is just these stories that almost destroyed, then saved him.
The lone wolf on the mountain top,
The wolf who'd bite off his own leg
Rather than be caught in a trap,
The wolf howl next to the cabin that sends chills down the spine.
Jack London's wolf, Farley Mowatt's wolf,
The Brothers Grimm to Zane Grey,
The list goes on and on.

But behind his bright and shining eyes
Is a better and older story
And no story at all.
Truth is, he's not the high plains drifting gunslinger
Of the animal world at all – he's a regular-guy kind of wolf,
A family man.
He marries one girl one time and stays with her for life.
He even lets her family move into the house with them,
And not just the close relatives,
All of them, including the crazy cousin nobody can stand.
He hangs out with his kids at their stinky little den
And teaches them stuff
When he'd rather be out with his buddies hunting elk,
Running down jackrabbits
And drinking from cool mountain streams.

Oh, sure he can eat a quarter of his own weight at one meal
But a guy's got to cut loose sometimes doesn't he?
How much pizza can you eat
Watching bad Monday Night Football?
And yes, he can get surly with uninvited guests
Like when you're trying to fix the sink
And the Jehovah's Witnesses knock on the door.
And I'll give you the fact that he gets a little nuts
Under a full moon, just like you when you were 16,
Drinking sloe gin and out with your first girlfriend.
But generally he prefers cooperation to chaos,
A pattern to rugged individualism.
Hell, he'll even get by on voles for supper
Rather than invade his neighbor's back yard.

And all the time the younger guys
Are lurking out on the edge of the family circle
Just waiting for him to slip up a little,
To lose a few seconds coming off the mark
To have his hairline recede a little more with the mange.
Like an aging action-adventure movie star
Still doing his own stunts at 60,
Or the old heavyweight
Who can still drop you with that sneaky right hand.
It's hard to give up that Alpha spotlight.
If we didn't admire and fear him so much
He wouldn't be teetering on the edge
Of The Endangered Species List.
He'd have been rubbed out of existence
Just like all the lesser animals we don't think of
As Noble or Mythic or Emblematic of a spirit we once had,
That we still touch in dreams,
And that somewhere along the way, for whatever reason,
We sold down the river.

N. A. F. T. A.

The lanky snowmobiler squatting next
To the brokedown Arctic Cat
In a side pass of the Canadian Shield
Looks like a young William Holden.
His goggles are cobbled with duct tape,
His knuckles thick-fleshed with scar tissue.
Gauze threads matted into bloody creases
Of his bar-fighter's hands dangle
Like puppet strings dipped in merlot.

But his smile is resplendent
As he mimes the exploits
Of his recent New Year's Eve damage.
After we have skied past my host tells me
He's a good man gone to booze.
"So, he guzzles his family's food money
And the children are on the province's dole, then."

That night – under a garish full moon –
The temperature 26 below,
We snowshoe miles into the hills,
Watch wolves cavort
On the far bank of an icy river.

All the while I am thinking
Of a moonlit night years ago
And another thin man
Kneeling next to a statue of the Blessed Virgin
In the Plaza del Centro of a small island
Off the Yucatan Peninsula. He was offering up
His naked baby to me, saying:
"Colosio esta muerto.
Llevla al Norte.
No puedo cuidarla."

In Michigan I teach the emotionally impaired
At a school next to the city's sewage plant.
The kids joke about trading punches with stepfathers
And putting out the eyes of kittens.

The wolves of Canada are beautiful
And the martyrs of Mexico
Have bled the ground red.
In time, some of my students
May read of them.

THE LAST DAY OF THE YEAR

The old saying goes: "Play like you'll live forever,
Pray like you'll die tomorrow."
But what if it wasn't just the last day of the year?
What if it really was the last night of the world,
The last day of your life?
How would you spend it?
With whom and why?
Obviously impractical questions,
Given the depth and breadth of your all-consuming life.
But isn't that just how we fool ourselves moment after moment?
Suffering fools, getting by, making do, living in the now,
Setting aside for the rainy day, which when it comes
Washes away more than our sins and foibles.

Let me tell you some stories to illustrate.
For five years I lived in a house once occupied by a famous artist.
Everything he ever painted or collected was still there.
Ten thousand vinyl records, classical and jazz,
Books enough to fill a library, stacked chest-high everywhere,
Huge mural-sized paintings in the basement,
In rented storage bins, the porch, attic, and barn.
A lifetime of copious accumulation and defense
Against the dread of a life ill-spent.
And of course his day of reckoning came and went,
The world turned a new page, calendar fluttered and moved on.
Somewhere along the line his love of things became cancerous
And he starved to death in his gluttony.

I once sat in the office of an old teacher of mine,
Watched him fill the room with plumes of pipe smoke,
Back when you could smoke indoors,
Listened to him rage against the machine,
Wax poetic on virtue and vice,
Embellish and elaborate on subjects great and small.
Finally after hours he turned to me and said:
"You know what Ph.D. stands for, don't you?
Piled high and deep."
At least he knew his place in the cosmic food chain.
And what of the Buddhist ascetic who says:
"If you have a bowl and a blanket,
You're carrying too much in life."
The trouble with most teachers? They require an audience.
The trouble with students? They're conditioned to receive.

I would spend the last-of-all-days outside.
Not re-reading the masters, but looking at clouds.
I'd burn my little stack of money, listen to the wind,
Watch trees bend and sway.
I'd write three letters, cry a little, laugh a lot,
Remember and forget.
I'd like to think I wouldn't beg for more time,
But probably would.
Wouldn't have regrets, but probably would.
Would forgive my transgressors, but probably wouldn't.
Would be satisfied, but probably wouldn't.

I'd like to think I'd be resigned, benign and stoic.
Truth to tell, I'd probably be pissed
And petty and simpering.
And some part of me
Would be making some small plan for the future.
Let us cross over the river together
And rest in the shade of the trees.

He had mended halyards
Early in the morning
Hand-rubbed linseed
Into the keel for the third time
In the afternoon
And now with evening
Propped the smooth board next to the woodstove
Where sawdust filmed over the tacky finish
In seconds
Tall grasses writhed and lay dying
In the backyard
Between patchwork heaps
Of old snow
As he stood looking out the window
At a procession of stars and clouds

Spitting
Drawing on a cigarette
Putting tools away
He thought of cutthroats and steelhead
Pulling against current
Returning to the sandbank
Where the DNR
Had dumped them
From the back
Of a three-quarter-ton pickup
The place where
Without knowing how or why
They would return
Spawn and die

In the night he walked to the lake
Knelt to the brackish wash
Knew the same furious calm
The power all water has
Over things alive

Tomorrow he would cast oarlocks
Curse the hoarfrost
Strike out for the longshoring docks
When the moon waxed
Feel his muscles tighten
Waiting for another season
And another

The Potential of Probability

"how small the news was …
a permanent change had come …

– Charles Olson

There was a time when I thought you hung the moon.
When the world spanned out before us
Like raindrops and bread dust.
When we would have all we wanted just because we wanted it.
In the small village of industry and assiduity
We were the king and queen.
But life is not constructed
To pay homage to our vagaries and vanities.
It wasn't new what happened.
These stories play out all the time.
Wind pushes the moon,
Something drifts across your heart
And love succumbs to that which is not expedient.
So the doom came and worlds stopped for a while.
And because this is the way it works,
You either die or become stronger.
For a long time I was dead.
Then a leaf fell across the path on some walk I'd taken
Because I couldn't stand to be alone in that house
And the sun on the leaf and the smell of the woods
And the possibility of love welled up
And the earth turned again, albeit slowly.
I wish it were simpler than that, or more complex.
But mostly reaction is like this: one step and then another.
Someone stands in a doorway and waves
And you remember it forever.
Rain falls on a summer afternoon as the sun breaks cloud cover
And a rainbow appears, if only for an instant and then is gone.
The circle wobbles, fails, reconnects itself as music and longing.

From that world of memory and blisters
    squeezed like sweat through shoes,
I emerged a hull with frayed muscle,
    tattered as dead rabbits tossed on the metal
Barn roof. Plodding after his chores,
    strewn with gestures of contempt,
Ineffective as shadows moving over dirt.

On his land, with every furrow thumbnailed true,
    I blustered, furred with velvet mold
Like the center of a nightcrawler carton left
    in the sun or thickly ungeometric
As ants working a watermelon rind,
    the sticky residue of his opinions
Clinging like grease to motor parts.

So I made for a tangled track outward
    to where his boundaries ended
And the grim rise of the sun across
    sectioned hillsides staked a less even path.
Where wind came through blackened grass
    skittering on its own accord
And living things in fields bore no brand marks.

Just after 7 a.m. CDT on the morning of July 4, 1999, a mesoscale convective weather system originated over the western plains of the United States of America. This synoptic storm environment featured an excessively warm air mass ceiling at 700 millibars which formed a cap, trapping low level moisture and cold air at 500 millibars, and was fed by a massive induced rear-inflow jet of cold air. Forty miles west of Fargo, North Dakota, the intensifying storm altered its course to the north-northeast, accelerated in speed and launched out on a direct heading toward Ely, Minnesota.

Shortly after 9 a.m., The Doppler radar station in Duluth observed two separate deep in-flow notches begin to feed the storm, resulting in an effect known as a bow echo.

The storm pattern struck Ely with wind speeds of 55 mph just as the 4th of July paraders were gathering. The wind collapsed booths at the park and blew over a tree that tore open the roof of a Chapman Street house. After passing through the town, the storm accelerated dramatically as rapidly intensifying convective elements merged at the northern edge of the storm. Over the next 48 minutes, sustained wind speeds reached 87 to 93 mph, resulting in an unknown amount of destruction of plant and animal life and habitat. The swath of the bow echo flattened 600 square miles of the Boundary Waters Canoe Area Wilderness, or approximately 400,000 acres. The National Weather Service officially categorized this event as only a "class two storm".

There is a wind from Morocco, the Aajej, against which the Fellahin defend themselves with knives. There is the Ghibli from Tunis, which produces a strange nervous condition in all that encounter it. And then there is the Harmatton, called the sea of blood. Red sand from this wind has flown as far as the southern coast of England and produced showers mistaken for blood. Herodotus writes about a wind, the Simoon, which a nation thought so evil they declared war on it.

The wind never blows so cold in this life
As when it crosses an open field,
An empty heart, a broken soul.

I knew a man who drank a case of beer every night
Just so he could sleep.
Knew a woman who was bulimic for twenty years
Because it was the only thing in her life she could control.
I had a friend who wrote such complicated, textured music
He could never finish a song, or if he did,
Couldn't play it and thus could never fail.

I also knew a woman who thrived at everything she did.
Perfect and graceful on the earth, nuanced and strong,
She told me once she'd rather live with hope than realization.
An 'old soul' beyond her years.
Her life was shattered several times
And she'd gather up the tatters, mend the tears and move on.
Until her luck went south and her porcelain life shattered.
The point being: We are all works in progress,
Tossed and buffeted on the wind, which is our friend,
Which is our nemesis, which is our life.
A bullet point on an agenda
Someone scrolls past in some meeting without comment.

There's an abandoned mine I pass every day on my walk.
And ducking out of the rain one afternoon,
I hid in the toolshed doorway,
The wind vaulting in from the top of the world,
Ground shaking from thunder,
The hollow earth reverberating below my boots.
I turned to peek into a broken window,
And though no one had worked there in decades
There was a red exit sign lighted at the back door.
Who was it intended for?
Perhaps the souls of miners still trapped in the earth.
Perhaps some vestigial light left over
From a time when people cared.
Perhaps it was a guide,
Pointing the way to anything looking to flee,
Up and out and away. And into the wind.

There is no creation man has wrought upon this planet,
No machine, no idea, no dogma
To equal the wind.
No story or prayer or philosophy.
We cannot make anything that is its equal.

The larva of the common lacewing, which slithers
   and gorges until metamorphosis,
   controls the spread of aphids.
Wolfing down bugs seems a strange occupation
   to be viewed serviceable,
   but we judge most things
   by their lesser of two evils quality.

So I'm packing all my ugly clothes again,
   a lackey to the job. Moving up.
   At forty-four, these moves are killing me,
   but I can't stay in one place, ravenous.
Lachesis – one of the Fates, the Greek goddesses
   who controlled the length of life –
   and her wyrd sisters, Clotho and Atropos,
   who spun and pruned its tendrils,
   are perched on the J&B boxes from the party store, laughing.
   They croon to me the folly of movement.

Even as I sort my sacred texts, culling a chapter here,
   puzzling a phrase there,
   I know they have taught me nothing;
   only the food and travel books hold any interest.
My one book of European history falls open
   to the tenth century: Nomads and feudal lords
   gleefully butcher each other, as bugs crawl over everything.
   Late in the century an interregnum period
   in one of the tiny provinces calms the fracas.
In the vacancy between abdication and ascension,
   peasants scurry for cover, root for food,
   fill their meager satchels with larder and move on.

He used to say when the shit came down
The trick was to think of yourself in the third person.
To step away and get perspective.
I'm sure the school board took that kind of talk
Into account when they ran him out of the district.

He used to say the world was made for taking chances.
That history was written only by the victors of wars
And that all politicians were genocidal necrophiliacs.
To bring up that fact when they fired him
He said would be beating a dead horse.
"Your schools are run by brood mares and geldings
standing in stud," he said. "Pun intended."

The union came to his defense
Till they heard his worldview.
Then they asked for a public retraction,
Adopted a holding position,
Dropped the countersuit and let him
Stew in his own juices.

He moved upstate and left us
To a succession of matronly widows,
None of whom we ever really thought of as teacher.

Once hauling driftwood
Up from the bottom
Of Hamlin Lake
For grandmother to sell
Out in front of the cottage
I lost my footing in the claybed
With a stump half way on the raft
Heard the wet oak limb
Thump my forehead
And watched whitecaps dance
Into bas-relief
Then blue-green parallax
With a muffled roar and trilling
And a weightless declivity

The arm that grabbed my hair
Hands that tore the T-shirt
From my neck
Lips pressing over mine
Were hers
After scolding
And pressing egg yolk
Into the fistula
She fried bluegills
In beer batter
Served them on a bed tray
With two fingers
Of my first whiskey
And stayed up all night
Putting cubes in the icebag
Checking my pupils
Singing every song I loved
Over and over
Waking me every fifteen minutes
To see that I wasn't dead

"He came to believe that the useless journeys ...
were rather his misreadings of his own mood,
a duping of self with counterfeit expectations."

– William Kennedy

Why remember?
December is a vermin month,
Cold light, speechless clouds,
A month for sleepwalkers
And thick-bodied spiders climbing iced windows.

Snow now,
Bedeviling even quick thinkers,
Talkers like yourself
Who whisk meaning to the surface
By breaking glacial silences.
Who fill their cars with litter
And keep one shoe in the back seat until spring.
Small rebellions to squeeze the insignificant out.
Knowing the freeze and thaw of seasons
Will place the rest on proper ground.

This morning,
The coldest day of the year,
I walked out before sunup
To a pine grove
By a tree-crossed stream,
Startling a small herd of deer
With my crunch and bluster.
The stag froze at my approach
While the rest bolted down
Two sides of the knoll.
I faced him across
Twenty feet of indecision.
Twin vapors of a snort
And dull thud of his stamp
Echoed our shared language of equivocation.

And later,
Examining the icebound tracks
I saw that he had leaned both ways
Before remembering he was a deer
And should run.

My grandfather drove Canadian liquor
to the Blue Crystal Ballroom from Ludington,
picking it up from Capone's beer boats
coming down from Drummond Island,
meeting them two miles out in Lake Michigan
north of the Big Sable River
with a false-bottom Chris Craft.

Waiting for a fingernail smuggler's moon
to shove off from that famous dock
at the Fourth Ward pier,
my grandfather played Spit in the Ocean
and Faro with the help, and recited
Shelley's sonnet *Ozymandias* for the boys.

That was the place where he paid off
the railroad dicks and aldermen
to be gone every other Thursday night.
Where his flunkies Touchdown and Billy
matched jiggers of Old Crow and told jokes
about the Volstead Act, waiting for the old man
to return to help load the station wagon.
Where granddad tore up five C notes
and tossed them into the brackish wash
to convince the go-betweens
that this was a serious business.

Where Mayor Little Eddie O'Malley
and Monsignor Winoiecki drove down
together in Eddie's '09 Packard Landaulet
to pick up cases of Bushmills and Serbian brandy.
Where Hey Susie and Jenny-go-Lightly,
my grandfather's friends after Busha died,
waited in the bridgemaster's shack
smoking Chesterfield Kings,
painting their fingernails, yawning.

Where Half-Pint Davis, the middleweight golden glover,
KO'd Big Joshua, the black ham-and-egger heavyweight.
The last sanctioned bare-knuckle fisticuffs in Mason County.
Where thirty years later the scab oiler,
who got laid off from the city of Midland car ferry,
would shoot granddad through the neck
over eight dollars and some change.

I have spent a lifetime looking over my shoulder.
Made a whole career of woulda, shoulda, coulda.
Mined the past for every dollop of fool's gold
False promise – fits and starts.
I have loaded up my wagon
Time immemorial to dash headlong
Up a dry creek bed with a bogus treasure map,
Looking for anything that sparkled, shined or sang.

Perhaps it was my misspent youth or the fact that
My father died young and I didn't see the point.
Maybe I was just lazy or lacked internal fortitude.
Maybe the gene for righteousness was regressive in my soul.
Whatever the reason, whatever the rhyme,
The past always seemed to hold more promise
Than the future or the present.

I was the poster child of bad choices, wrong-headed schemes,
Misplaced alliances. Look up "self involved" in the dictionary,
You'd find my picture. Ask anyone on the street
About my character and they'd laugh in your face.
I never thought I'd live to see thirty
And my idea of long-term planning
Was to have enough beer for the weekend.
And then I changed, and I'll tell you how I did it.

I crashed a motorcycle, I lost someone I loved
And I walked on a beach for years.
The details are unimportant – private yet universal.
As common as dust and as glorious as a comet
Or the birth of your own child. As I write these lines,
This moment, it is another dark night, but there's a glimmer
Of refracted dawn in the east. It's almost tomorrow.

Fortune has a sliver in her eye.
The moon is low-slung.
Birdhouses full of seed husk.
The rain on pine cones
Or the cracking of tires
on almost frozen gravel
explodes a memory.
A car door slams
and someone
is back home again.

The first time you see
your breath this fall
you are looking
at pumpkins on a porch step;
maybe your sister is visiting,
singing in the house.
You hear the melody
but not the words.
There are rifle shots in the field.
If you have lived here a long time
you may know who is shooting,
even what has been shot.

Driving through Missouri one February day
About a week after an ice storm,
I watched Amish farmers clean up the downed branches
In all the yards with two-man bucksaws.
It was a scene of desolation and destruction
Unlike any I had ever seen.
And then I thought of Missouri's Favorite Son,
Harry Truman.
Give 'em hell Harry
The buck stops here Harry
The Show Me State's only President.
The only man in history to order the A-Bomb dropped –
Twice.

It would have looked like this on the morning after
In those two Japanese cities.
People who had nothing to do with the government
Out cleaning up that which would never be clean again.
And the Amish children that morning in Missouri,
In straw hats and bonnets, played in the chaos,
Piled sticks into bundles and laughed. It was a sunny morning.
They had the day off from school – they were children.

Abraham Lincoln once wrote: "If I could preserve the Union
Without freeing a single slave, I would."
Walt Whitman said: "The public is a thick-skinned beast
Which requires constant whacking."
You see, there never was a golden age
Of enlightenment in this country.
Everything we got, someone paid for.
Someone small and organized,
Someone the government said was an enemy, a traitor,
And a danger to society.
Someone who didn't understand how it works around here.

Years ago, I belonged to a Railroad Union.
To get a job with the railroad back then,
You had to go see Mr. Max, the union strawboss and president.
In the murky old union hall Mr. Max sat at his desk
Under a giant bas-relief mural
Of working men fighting with the railroad police.
Mr. Max would say: "I'm going to the bathroom now.
When I get back there had better be an envelope on my desk
With two hundred dollars in it
And you had better be gone." That's how it worked.
That's how it's always worked for people without clout.
When someone pushes, you push back.

The radio said, that February morning in Missouri,
That power would not be restored to some rural counties
For several more weeks.
But then again, why wouldn't the children be laughing?
The Amish don't have electricity.

GENIUS

They say the true genius of the world is its ability to adapt,
To transmogrify, to morph.
But, as they say, the devil is in the details.
In the Bible they gave us three choices: faith, hope and love.
Smart wasn't even in the equation.
Smart was the redheaded stepchild
No one liked when they wrote Corinthians.

But right now, somewhere among us, this second,
Is the smartest person in the world.
Perhaps it's just sheer number of brain cells,
Or maybe it's synaptic;
Their mind simply works better than others do.
Maybe it's discipline or intuition,
Or whimsy or fantastic connections.
Perhaps this person is so smart
That she never lets on to the rest of us.
Maybe he has secret meetings and handshakes
With other smart people,
Like the Masons, or the Knights of Columbus did
When I was little.

Perhaps we all start out as the smartest person
And then grow out of it,
Like wetting the bed or giving people the finger.
Maybe you only get to be the smartest for a day,
Maybe a few hours.
Maybe there are two smartest people
And they trade back and forth
So someone gets weekends off.

It's hard to think about the smartest person in the world
Having to shop for underwear, or clean off baby spit-up.
Maybe the smartest person in the world just always knows
Where their checkbook is, and the car keys
And where the winning lotto ticket will be sold.

Perhaps the smartest person in the world
Is the bum I stepped around in the doorway of the bus terminal
In Golden Gate Park, San Francisco three years ago,
Who looked up at me and asked for a dollar,
Then thanked me and said: "Anyone can have a job,
It takes talent and tenacity to be broke."

Maybe the smartest person in the world is a retired cartoonist
Who has never had her picture taken
Or been seen in public for years,
Who made millions of people laugh and cry
And ponder over her drawings and social critiques.
Who now lives in the mountains,
Down an old two-track driveway where she has a sign that reads:
"Please do not enter unless you've called."
But, of course, she has no phone.

Or maybe the smartest person in the world is a small child
Living in squalor in some Untouchable Caste System
Whose understanding of mathematical Chaos-String Theory
Dwarfs even that of Einstein's and Oppenheimer's.
Doing ciphering people will discuss for a thousand years.
And this child sits in a little hut all day long
Working out new distribution allocation models
For renewable resources,
Projected along unconventional lines of demarcation,
Just to ensure that no child
Anywhere, ever again, has to sit in the same situation.

I talked to a man last week who is 93.
I asked him how he's lived so long
And he told me it isn't the how anymore, it's the why.
He said it's in the blood. You either got it in you or you don't.
He said his father lived to 97
And that he was just hanging around
To beat the old man's record.
You're the radio guy aren't you, he said. Never forget a voice.
I can't remember my daughter's face or either of my wives,
But sounds I got down to a science.

Sounds don't lie.
You don't lift your inflections at the end of sentences
Like they do when they're trying to sell you something.
You can hear a lot if you listen to what's underneath the words.
I used to read a lot, everything. Eyes aren't any good anymore.
I started out listening, guess I'll end up that way.
As to your first question,
I grill a big steak once a week and eat it with ketchup,
Big glass of red wine every night before Jeopardy.

I used to know all the answers; now I don't know any.
That Trebeck guy knows all the answers though,
But he's got them written down for him.
Any more questions?
I don't have any answers
But I've been everywhere and back again, twice.
Yukon in the '30s for gold, South America for years for oil.
Lived in a cave in the Bitterroots once after the war.
Just for about six months
Till the sounds stopped ringing in my head.
Nice place when you got used to the bear smell.
You know what makes a cave? Time and water.
Come to think of it that's all I am anymore – time and water.

Viceroys will keep you going too.
I smoke one every night out on the porch if it isn't raining hard.
Got a nice kid brings me a pack every 20 days with the groceries.
I'm OK unless the month's got 31 days;
Then he gets confused and I have to wait a day,
At my age, though, you get used to waiting.
How many days does this month have?
This kid's wife makes a pretty good meatloaf on Fridays;
He brings along a hunk or two sometimes. Been to China too,
Almost went to Japan during the war, but they surrendered.

Seismology was my game.
Looking for oil you send down sound waves into the ground.
Sounds don't lie, did I say that before?
The earth doesn't lie either I suppose.
Guess I'll find out for sure soon enough when I'm in it.
Death doesn't scare me anymore –
Broken hip scares me and people who smile too much,
But death would be like going to a big party
Where all your friends are.
Nice girl from the V.A. comes to read to me, did you know that?
Stephanie, she's got a bad boyfriend and a pretty voice.
She's going to teach second grade. She'll be good at it too,
You can just tell about some people.

People don't normally talk to old folks – you must be lonely.
Old people are like the test star – you can't see them
If you look at them, you have to kind of look sideways.
You don't know what the test star is do you?
Before they had fancy equipment
Country folks would test their vision
By looking at the Dipper – big one I think.
Anyway just off the top of one of the stars in the handle
Is a little star you can only see if you kind of look away.
That's what old people are like I guess.

Say you want some coffee? I make a real good Brazilian coffee.
Or maybe it's time for a glass of wine.

There is a river I go to almost every day.
It is not wide and the current flows
Against the grain of the wind.
This river runs in consort with all my life.
There are never any people there –
Sound waves on an empty planet.

All fall the Sedge and Sage –
Lily Pads and Thicket Spurge
Fold their browning tent flaps
With delicious and fecund aromas.

The Great Herons no longer
Skitter down the freshet
Around the bend from the boat. Their stilted forms
Replaced by the thrum and basso profundo
Keenings of Canada Geese.
Block letter forms veering southward
As light tilts from a lessening angle.

Some mornings a dust of hoarfrost
Crystals the burrowing leaf track –
Making the tramp and tread
Alternately slick and adhesive.
One more corporeal season
Withering to the diffidence of time.
And I recall that
The dominant motifs of the universe
Are cold and darkness. The world reduced
To resplendent particulars.

In winter, like an auxiliary bloom at evening,
The river closes over. Currents not strong enough
To keep ice from forming. I ski into
The mouth of a U-shaped cleft in the frost pack and listen
To the Blue-Northern Coursers howling down upon all of us.
Sundogs, Black-Ice Outcroppings, Greenstone Erratics,
Stalks, Husks, Shards and Spikes – foundations
That hold the natural world together.

The sentinels and cathedrals of the smaller world
Of birds and insects, animals and fish
Whose calendar contains not weeks or months,
Not worry and wait,
Nor the cerebral wailings and gnashings of teeth,
Not the wringing of hands over unanswered prayers
That is so much a part of our lives,

Only the palpable sighs of the Omniscient Lords of Weather.
Only seconds and sensation, instinct and imagination.

Perhaps there is a rich and textured pattern to the world.
And yet, standing in the middle of our lives,
We cannot see it.
The intersecting lines of comfort and compulsion
Blur distinctions.
As if the compass held a fifth cardinal point – Chaos.

Years ago I was in love with a woman
Who believed in only one thing in life – Circles.
Yet when she drew out the parameters
I was on the outside.

Once, on a lake in the north,
I watched a Sandhill Crane work the shore and draws
Of a small marsh all afternoon –
Stand-wait-genuflect-strike.
In the fractured light of late October
It appeared a dance of design and necessity.

A famous writer told me years ago
That the only thing wrong with a long walk
Was that you had to turn around and go back home.
But isn't that the point?
Because even in retracing your steps
One never returns the same.

This morning at dawn, I sat on the porch
And watched a thousand tiny birds dart past the window,
Grouping to migrate.
Each one indistinguishable from the others,
Yet distinct and invaluable.
The warrant of the flock predicated on
The least social, the one most wary of the groups.

A decade ago I stood on a mountain in the Cascade Range
Watching the sun fall over four states,
The diminishing light setting on all of us,
Below and above equally.
And yet, it seemed the places the light struck
Were between people and their creations,
Between ourselves and who we wished to be,
Between all we value and ignore.
That light, which some would say was wasted,
That light was the most beautiful.

THE JUNIOR BARN

One of my chores on the ranch when I was a kid
Was to burn the papers and dump the trash each night
Out behind the little barn, one of three we had,
The one we called the junior barn.
As opposed to the senior barn
And the grandpa barn.
In an old 55-gallon drum
My dad got from the trainyard at the C&O Railroad,
I'd set the brown paper sacks
And try to crack a kitchen match on my thumbnail.

And one Christmas season more than forty years ago,
My father had to go to the hospital for an operation on his heart.
Some state a million miles away called Minnesota
In a place called the Mayo Clinic.
Our neighbor, old Jack Kraus,
Came over to help with the horses and one night said to me:
"I'm not going to B.S. you kid, your Dad's in a tight spot
And he may not make it.
You'd better start thinking like the man of the house.
Think about this stock here and your brothers and sisters."

We kept the stallions standing in stud
And the mean geldings in the junior barn,
Away from the mares and foals and the gentle day riders.
The junior barn was for roans and cribbers,
For the quarter horses and thoroughbreds who bit or kicked,
Who weren't saddle broke, halter trained, lunge-lined or polite.
It was where I felt the most at home
Of any place I've ever been in this life.

On Christmas Eve that season with the temperature 20 below,
I trudged out across the yard to burn the papers
Next to the sledding hill. Our two great champions,
Rainy-Day-Texas and Tag-Along-Downhill,
Stood in the corral in a frozen stupor
Beneath their horse blankets and frosted eyelids, watching me.
I can still see the twin plumes of their breath
Almost reaching the ground,
Still hear the trees in the woods
Pop and crack in that freezing night air,
Still smell the fetid, rank odor coming from the open barn door.

I remember dropping to my knees in the snow
To pray for my father
Next to that burning can of papers behind the junior barn.
I remember seeing a small red fox run up the hill.
I remember clouds parting and moonlight glinting
Off the ice of the Lincoln River in the front pasture.
I remember the warm breath of those two mean horses
On my head and, for the life of me,
I'll remember till the day I die
That the hand of God passed over me that night
Almost half a century ago.

In the hospital that evening my father fought for his life.
A rejection fever had set in
And they put him in an ice bath to bring down his temperature.
Years later my Grandmother told me he never made a sound.
He just looked at the doctors and nurses with dark, shining eyes
And nodded his head when they talked to him.
He recovered and lived another decade, another ten Christmases.
Five years ago I went back to that place
For the first time in decades.
Nothing was the same; everything looked smaller, stranger.
But then, I suppose, God never stays in one place very long.

Of course they're not really stars at all, the falling ones.
But they do crash into us
Because the Earth pulls everything down eventually
And maybe not in the way you're thinking.
If Angels really did get their wings every time a bell rang
Or a star fell that would be sweet, but, truth to tell,
It's all just stuff floating around in space
Till we mythologize it.
Just like us, I guess.
That doesn't mean we shouldn't wish on them
Or that they're not a sign or omen.
They are if we wish them to be so.

But a person can spend a lifetime waiting to be gifted
And never see the truth,
That we build up the world new each and every day.
Blessing those things we honor and hold sacred,
Fighting through the tedium of another Tuesday at work,
And occasionally
Touching something so remarkable within ourselves
We're left speechless,
Blinking in disbelief that we could have
Made such beauty in the world.
And if it helps to believe in pretty stories
About a just and merciful God,
Stories about wishing on stars,
Pulling a wishbone apart with a friend,
Well, more power to you, whatever gets you through the night,
Any port in a storm, Katie bar the door, too wet to plow, etc.

I wrote a line once in a poem many years ago:
"Anyone's life can be legendary; all you have to do
Is every once in a while do something legendary."
I think I stole that line.
But we all steal and borrow and take from this world
What we need to make sense.
What you do every day, what makes up your life
Is as important as any president or doctor or saint.
And there really is more truth in an idea
Than in all the parsing words in any book
Of philosophy or prophecy.
Which is the hand of God,
Which our minds invent,
Which comes from the celestial cosmos,
Which our brain interprets every moment –
Well, you get the point.

And the falling stars around us,
The romantic ones with the tragic flaws,
The missing parts, the broken pieces,
The ones just here for a moment or two,
They're special because we need them to be so.
Because as they flame and flash across the night sky of our lives,
We see in them our own impermanence and importance.
And sometimes, sometimes,
When we hitch our wagons to these falling Angels,
It's because it's the right thing to do.

I was thinking tonight of a shoreline
When your face came to me.
Only it wasn't your face today;
It was your face years ago.
Before husband, house or job
When your laughter circled
Higher with possibility.

When you came south I fled.
Gone to a fable which ended up
As life in the north.
Now you are home and I've moved
Three times in a year.
Now you grind rich, oily coffee beans
And race from project to project,
As if from child to child and your family
Is a sequence of performances,
Each squealing: "Look at me,
Look at me."
You doubt each risk
Yet are glad for the work.

You say you are happy
And I believe you really are.
You say your house is life
And I truly think it is.
You say you love a man
And I know you do, deeply.
You say you love the land
And its continuations.
Yes, I can see you have
Found a fertile place.

You wear plum-colored clothing
And still enjoy a snap of brandy
In your mouth and sleep better
And better, sometimes all night.

But walking into your kitchen
I see dusty sunlight on packed boxes
And hats piled upon themselves
And a gypsy wagon waiting
Out by the hummingbird feeder
And I know you want to run.
To dance with strangers in linen suits
On beaches with Latin names.
To edge out into water naked
With someone mysterious in a sunset
Far from your beautiful home.
Your well-formed mouth
Licking oysters, your umbrella
Turned inside-out in a wind
Which has traveled a thousand miles
In an afternoon.

Champagne and whispers
Instead of poison sumac.
Dreams instead of territory.
Mirrors instead of windows.

A humid, exotic movie
You walk to on your own terms
With dry feet.

Maybe there was a man walking
    in and out of sight
passing over and down hills
    coming your way
never waving but seeing you
    from a long way off
and knowing you so well
    as to be sure you would stay
until he was in earshot
    and even longer cause
you were from the same stock
    and it wasn't polite to yell at folks

maybe he was your father
    and you had screwed up again
the long walk out to your spot
    had cooled him and
he didn't have to slap you
    just stand over the stump
you leaned against
    shake his head
let his breath catch up
    and then say something important
that you would remember even after he
    was dead
then say supper was on
    that you both would be late
and there would be hell to pay

maybe this could have happened
    but it didn't
maybe we invent our fathers
    every day until we have the nerve
to invent ourselves

maybe the hills should cover these myths
    and we could go to a new well and
draw something fresh
    something fluid

Four Jokes About Control

It takes so much energy to run someone else's life.
And I'll grant you the fact
That humans have been striving for structure and order
Since we hobbled out of the primordial ooze.
But what has that given us in the long run,
Besides distance learning, cell phones,
And the Home Shopping Network?

I knew a therapist once who, in addition to saving my life,
Would say pithy things like: "I'm not big on control issues,
It's like the captain of the Titanic running around
Counting the deck chairs."
It's like the old joke that goes: Knock knock. Who's there?
Control freak – OK, now you say control freak who.
And our opinions are like armpits –
We all have them and we all think our own don't stink.

Even our cousins the animals are not immune.
A DNR officer once told me that
The most common way beavers die is that,
In attempting to manipulate their habitat,
They drop trees on themselves.
How many beavers could have been saved
With a little less neurosis?
But beavers have to chew or their teeth get so long they can't eat.
What's our excuse: boredom, repressed guilt,
Misplaced anger management?

Ultimately control fails
Because of the very nature of the universe itself.
The hand that rocks the cradle in this deal
Is randomness and diversity
Yet, somehow, in the miasma of chaos theory there is structure.

Let me offer this exemplar:
A woman I used to know asked me to bury her dog.
The dog had been the loving pet of her dead father
And she didn't have the heart to do the job.
She told me to take him out in the woods
Because he loved to play in the woods, and just pick a spot.
I chose a place beneath an apple tree in an abandoned orchard,
Dug down several feet and, by chance, struck a ceramic jar.
The jar contained the ashes of the woman's father,
Which she and her brother had placed there years before.
The cosmos brought them back together.

And, oh yes, the fourth joke about control.
A comedian I admire once said:
Men want the same thing from women
That they want from their underwear –
A little support and a little freedom.

An Inventory of Personal Assets

I'd like to administer, today, a little test.
However, this is not a test you can fail – then again,
You can't pass it either.
This test consists of one question and a universe of responses.
It's a one-time-only, bargain-basement, discount-close-out,
Hold-the-phone, how-can-they-offer-prices-like-that
Assessment of your personal character.
And who else's character are you really interested in anyway?

Ready? Here we go. You wake up one night and,
God forbid, your house is on fire.
You get all the loved ones and the pets out,
And now you have twenty seconds
To save one personal belonging.
(Does this sound like the test where you choose
Between the sick, old lady and the priceless work of art?
Well it is and it isn't.)
So, twenty seconds, one thing – what's it going to be?
OK, GO, and ...
Time's up, pencils down, what's your answer?

Congratulations, you qualify for the second round of questions,
Where the prize money doubles and your mortal soul's at stake.
But seriously, what did you pick, and why?
What made this one item the most important, that is,
Superceded all the rest?
And what does this choice say about you?

For me it's an old book,
The 1938 Webster's Unabridged Dictionary.
It is seven inches tall and weighs nine pounds.
It contains the collected wisdom
Of a thousand years of human life.
Before technology, there were books.

An old farmer named Merritt Fox
Gave me this book a quarter century ago.
The only time we ever spoke,
Though we were neighbors for years.
He was ancient by then, well into his nineties,
And one afternoon he walked across my yard,
Staggering under the weight of a package, and said:
"I hear you're a writer, you might want to take a look at this."
Then he left.
I tried to return the book a week later, thinking it only a loan,
But his wife met me at the door,
Said he'd died and maybe I should keep it.

The things we have in this life, the things precious to us,
Sometimes come unexpectedly from places we never imagined,
From people we hardly know, and then they're gone
And we wish we could have spent more time with them,
Or any time with them.
Take children, for example.
They pass through our lives like freight trains.
One second you're holding a helpless thing,
The next they're driving away,
Leaving a swirl of dust, a heart full of memories,
And if we're lucky, very lucky,
One thing, one thing.

Anzio

Lost on a back country road I stop at a fruit stand
For directions and strawberries.
The couple behind the table
Are the oldest human beings I have ever seen.
We talk about the weather, their lives, mine, and then
They invite me for a glass of iced tea.
As they rise and move across the yard
They lock arms and appear as one leathery, four-legged animal.

In the house their possessions are as old as they.
Over here a china doll from another century,
Over there a sword from the Civil War.
"That was my father's," the old man says,
But he could not possibly be that ancient.
In the kitchen we gather glasses and wedges of lemon
And walk out the back door.
The steps are spongy, almost giving way.
In the backyard they have arranged lawn chairs
In a row facing the garden
And we sit down to watch the beans grow
And listen to the sprinkler hiss and spit.

The day is stifling and even though
I'm wearing only shorts and a T-shirt
I pour sweat.
The old man is wearing a flannel shirt, wool pants,
And slouch hat of no color at all,
And looks perfectly cool and relaxed.

"So you're a writer," the old woman says. "My son was a writer.
I want to show you something."
She leaves and is gone a long time.
I look up at the lightning rod on the top of the barn
And the blue breaker ball is so old
The sun has burned it chalk white.
The old man says nothing for so long that after a while
I think he might have died.
But then he erupts a huge wad of tobacco spit into the garden.
"Good for the cut worms," he says and laughs.

When the old woman returns
She presses a folded square of paper into my hand
And as I unwrap it the paper is so old
Bits fleck away and fall to the dirt.
But the words at the bottom of the note are unscathed
And they are remarkable.
It says: " Sometimes love is like a young mother
Trying to take a knife away from a child.
No matter how you go at it,
Eventually you just have to reach in and hope for the best."
"My son wrote that a long time ago," she says.
"I always thought it should be in a story.
He died in World War II, at Anzio in January 1944.
We found it on a map in the National Geographic."
And then no one speaks for a long time
And I think about this boy who wanted to write,
But instead died on an Italian resort beach at age nineteen.
Finally I ask them to tell me their story.

"We were farmers," the old woman says,
"Hoosiers – Brown County, Indiana, sixty-one years,
But the farm got to be too much and the kids didn't want it,
So we moved here. It's cold in the winter.
We write letters, the old man makes birdhouses, I knit,
But at our age it's mostly about loss."

I then ask my question: "So, how old are you two?"
"One hundred and seven," says the old man.
"Born the same day, same county – different families though,
Like she said, we're Hoosiers, not from Kentucky,"
And he laughs so hard his teeth come loose.

After a while I say my goodbyes and as I rise to leave
The old man grabs my wrist as I pass and whispers:
"I have something important to tell you."
I bend down so low that my ear almost touches his hat.
"Put the money for the strawberries in the can on the table,"
And again he laughs.

And that is just what I do when I walk back to my car.
Then I turn to look back to the garden across the yard
Filled with burdocks and timothy
And I cannot tell if they are still there or if they ever were.
But when I walk over to the car
I see that the old woman has loaded zucchinis
And sprigs of Indian paintbrush with tiny purple ribbons
Into the backseat.

I drive away and for a long time I see neither people nor farms
And it's then that I realize I never got directions from them.
But I think, sometimes when we are most lost,
Something reaches out to us and shows us the way.

I stop at a gravel four-way and clouds of dust billow into the car
And just for a second I disappear.
Then I pick a direction at random
And drive for a long time.

They were gandydancers
Who had worked for the railroad forty years.
They told tales
Of when they used to tamp the ties by hand
And of the mudslides of the Appalachia
And of Lother Swan who'd lost his foot
To some double-edged crossing switch
That somebody had forgotten to trip up
On the B&O line
Or the Chesapeake and Ohio
Or some TVA project.

They used to come up from West Virginia
To my grandparents' cottage to fish for the summer.
They were hard men, it goes without saying,
But they laughed a lot and they told strange stories
About women that I pretended to understand
And they never went to church.
They used to let me finish the Carling Red Cap Ale
Dead soldiers from their card tables
And when my grandparents would finally fall asleep
I'd sneak out to the cottage and watch Ernie Kovacs
On the big Zenith they'd brought up
In the back of their Airstream
And there was Snooky Lawson singing
"Red Sails In The Sunset."
And one night when I'd eaten
Too many of the pickled mountain oysters
And was out by the boathouse tossing my cookies into the lake
Old Red came up behind me
And as he knelt down to where I was
I heard his limber legs crack at the knee.
He picked me up in those forearms thick as oak stumps
And pitched me into the lake and laughed
And I laughed too.

I remember they caught snapping turtles
The big ones
The thirty pounders
The ones you swore you saw
When you went skinny dipping late at night.
Well they'd fix their dead-bolt eye hooks
Into the breakwater where we would throw the fish heads
And bend grappling hooks
With huge channel locks from their tool boxes.
They always had a lot of turtle soup
And used the shells as ashtrays
For their Luckies and Chesterfields.
They drove big green Hudsons
With wide whitewall tires.
They used to let me clean the Y bones
Out of their northern pike
And pluck the pearls from the sheephead late at night
Under the yellow bug light
While they played Canasta and Spit In The Ocean
Snapped each other with wet towels
And pumped up their railroad lanterns.

My grandmother sold off the place after Ed died.
She couldn't keep up the taxes
And I went back a few years later to look it over.
The man who bought it
Was an undersheriff from Houghton Lake
Who'd fly his family over weekends
In a big twin prop seaplane.
He remembered me from my football days.
Standing there in a grove of birches
I'd helped my grandfather plant thirty years before
I watched him use a pneumatic sand blower
To sink new steel corrugated pylons
For the superstructure of the dock.

Out there in his hip waders
His magenta jacket
And those funny sunglasses with a chain around the neck
He dredged up an old cedar board
With a rusted eye hook in it
And said: "What the hell is this?"
As he sluiced it over the top of the lake to me
I knelt down to peer into the water
And as I did I heard my knees crack
And I smiled and squinted up into the sun
To see them all standing there again on the dock
With their tattoos
And their faded canvas trousers
And those funny red leather caps
With the hand-tied leaders
And silver spoons
And the shiny Dardevles in the brim.
They were gandydancers
Who had worked for the railroads for forty years
But they're all dead now.
A whole way of living gone.
And nobody much remembers them anymore
Except me
And now you.

GIFT

Six times in as many years
  Accidents happened to my people
Falls from haylofts
  Thistle shard raked an eyeball
Cinch strap looped back asswards
  Flayed out at full gallop
Knives axes power tools skived into bone
  Country folks far from doctors
Mark time in blood spills and
  Fractures
Grandma had a bent
  For calling these before they happened
I got the owning
  The edge   the shine   the vision
Whatever
From that gnarled old woman

Standing with her in the garden
  Twisting tomato bugs
She soured up her face
  Said harshly
"Cain't call it no gift
  Useless to know
When there ain't nothin
You can do"

I used it though
  On women
Fishing
  In school
Whenever it came around
  Warning of a terrible
A reckless
Or a valuable encounter

And that summer in the late '50s
  Holding the forked ends
Of a water witch with Uncle Cleave
  Leaning into the hill
Watching the business end
  Dance and wiggle at cowflop
And joe pie weeds
  Seeing as he turned swallowed and accepted
Not magic
Necessity

In the new spring
  I watch the horses run.
  All that muscle across
  the frozen grass. And
  I turn to see my boys'
  faces hidden in their
  winter coats. Laughing
  with red cheeks. And there
  is something in the light
  or the way in which it falls
  that you know the winter is
  over.
It is always at this time
  that I am glad that I
  have lived and grown
  to see the strange
  way in which I do.
One season starting,
  one ending. I look hard
  at my kids' faces and
  decide not to cry.
So in the new spring
  hell
  I might even stop and
  smile.

A torn, weathered hand
moves along a brocade
lifted from the chest
of catarrh air and peptic time.
Ribald cigarette smoke and phlegm-covered skin.
Macrame.
Disease.

Stockings droop, eyelids, cataracts.
Wine from a heavy silver teaspoon.
The omniscient radio.
Clocks.
Terrible
shoes.

Mortar bowels, morphine,
the rattle of inclement laughter.
Hip pointers, liver spots, emery board tongue.
That which was an elbow, face, woman.
Facsimile.
Nemesis.
Jezebel.

A dream in exile,
the young prince forsaken.
A waltz in crinoline with lost slippers on wet summer lawn.
The huge sin of kissing.
That sheen of braided hair in sunlight.
Waves.
Cambric.
Mist.

THE PHILOSOPHERS

A woman I greatly admire said to me recently
That one would have to be a fool not to see
the hand of God in all of this.

Well, I am a fool, and I don't believe in God
Just the goddess – or if some single deity –
Then perhaps the god of Wittgenstein or Spinoza
Who rolled the cosmic tumblers, set the works in motion
And then sat back to see if we could figure out the math.

But Wittgenstein gave away his family's fortune
To work in a rose garden – to dwell in utter poverty.
He said that language was a trap which kept people
From saying what they meant.

And he published only one book in his lifetime,
A thin volume: *Tractatus Logico Phiosophicus.*
He said that life was beautiful and methodical
And musical and logical – and then he shocked the world
By saying he could prove it.

Well, I am not a great philosopher, just a minor regional poet.
And there is almost nothing in my life I can prove.
But there are several things I know.

In this world the only thing more enigmatic than a
Hopeless romantic is one who has remained hopeful.
And the precipitous fall which some of us encounter
Avails us of several opportunities for learning.

The first is the infinite variety which coupling can take,
And the second, the more important lesson,
The "other" is the almost unlimited chance for redemption.
For like the Phoenix rising out of the ashes
We can reinvent ourselves and start again.

Like Icarus tumbling out of the sky
In that Breugel painting we all so dearly love,
Until we love ourselves enough to ask, in this world
No one really notices or cares.

Thoreau wrote: "The mass of men lead lives
Of quiet desperation."
And Plato said: "That in life which we love most dearly
Eventually destroys us."

Well, I don't mean to be disingenuous, but I for one
Shall go laughingly to my grave extolling the virtues,
The awe and majesty of the only thing
For which we should live and die: Love.

And not the blind staggers of some romantic
Version of love sold to us by a culture which honors nothing
Except profit and humiliation, but a more pragmatic view,
Like two tall trees standing equal under the sun,
Where the roots are intertwined feeding nutrients to each other.
Two trees standing so that the shade of both harms neither.

Now I know this kind of love can exist and you say to me
That's all well and good, so prove it.
And I say that I cannot.

You have to take it on faith alone.
The faith, the Bible says, of the mustard seed.
And you have to look to nature, for in nature
As in all things, you find the proof of it.

October Snowstorm

I was watching my neighbor shoveling snow off his porch
And I was laughing.
I was laughing because my neighbor isn't very nice
And I don't like him and I was glad he was having a hard time
Getting all that snow off his porch.
As you can probably tell already he and I don't get along.
We have differing worldviews and other problems
Like barking dogs and loud mufflers and too many visitors
When I'm trying to get some work done and need it to be quiet.

I was watching my neighbor shoveling snow off his porch
And I was thinking
I'm going to have to do something soon about all these problems
He and I have. He is not the kind of person
You can reason with, real set in his ways, as they say.
He probably doesn't stay up most of the night like I do,
Trying to solve the problems of the world
Through metaphysical poetry and advanced intelligence.
He probably just sits in his lounge chair
And lets television wash all over him, has a couple of drinks
And sleeps like a baby all night, the rat.

He is having a difficult time with all that snow now
Because of an indolent and inactive lifestyle.
Not like me, always out early riding my bike
Or skiing or hiking or doing other proactive, interesting,
Positive things to prolong my youthful appearance and vitality.

Well, maybe not every morning; sometimes I lie in bed
Until eleven or twelve or so, but only if I've been up late
Solving important world problems
Or having to worry about jerks like my next door neighbor.
Come to think of it, if I wasn't such a pacifist
I could do a guy like that great bodily harm.
Who do people like that think they are?

He probably stays up all night playing on the Internet,
Figuring out how to make even more money
Than he already has, which is a lot,
Judging by all the toys he has in his yard.
He probably just invented yet another way
Of screwing people over in Indonesia or some other country
Where they make you work thirty hours a day for like 22 cents.
He probably thinks the poor deserve to be poor.
That they don't have any initiative or gumption.
That they are what's wrong with the world
Instead of guys like my neighbor.

But right now he isn't so high and mighty is he?
Right now I bet he wishes he hired someone to clean off his porch.
To get rid of the mess that this storm has brought down on him.
Right now I bet he wishes he were anyone but who he is:
A fat, rich, hungover Internet tyrant with a beer gut,
A shovel full of wet snow, a yard full of barking dogs
And some weirdo, poet, peacenik neighbor
Who's too damn lazy to get out and clean off his own porch.

Now I get it.
A man walks into a bar with a parrot on his shoulder.
A salesman stops at a farmer's house late at night.
Two women meet for lunch every day for a year
To chat about how bad their husbands are.
A couple of dogs are talking about their masters.
It's not in the punchline, or even in the timing –
Subject matter is unimportant
Or even who is the butt of the joke.
Humor, all humor I think, comes front loaded long before.
It has everything to do with empathy,
A willingness to extend your humanity.
It is programmed – or not – into the child
As defense against a cold,
Uncaring world, or is the product of imaginative unreasoning.

The *Sturm und Drang* of life balanced with wit and whimsy
And a willingness to pratfall over the misplaced footstool
In the dark night of the soul.
Some would say it's the surprise ending, the unintended pun,
The play of words on the tongue,
Some essential commonality of experiences we all share.
The half-truth, the sidelong glance, someone's dignity defiled,
Somebody put in their place, a secret revealed.
It's about being alive in the madness
And has something to do with joy.

Because to laugh or to cry is the same release in the long run.
And you get to choose so little in this life
Except how you view the world.
Cosmic joke or the dry, brittle realization
That every day's a Tuesday,
Every night a small death and then rebirth.
Laughter helps heal the world the way food stanches hunger,
The way reason eventually defeats greed,
The way kissing a child's scraped knee
Makes the pain go away.
It only works if you allow yourself to believe in the magic.

Or perhaps the greatest joke of all,
The one we play on the whole universe,
Is that we all still love each other
In the face of everything we know.

A man walks into a bar with a parrot on his shoulder
And says to the bartender . . .

My ex-wife used to collect shiny things,
More like an obsession than a collection really.
And I already know what you're thinking:
Ex-wife – obsession, etc. It's going to be
One of those kinds of poems, full of the post mortem dissections
Of someone's character with pithy little asides
To make the author appear morally superior,
More spiritually connected, more attuned with the cosmic,
Psychic lever and fulcrum.
A piece full of bile and vitriol and victimization.

Well, surprise, surprise – it's not going to be that kind of deal.
Truth is, we are all attracted to some kind of pretty shiny thing.
Spangle, babble, trinket, chochkey, keepsake,
Call it what you will.
And maybe it isn't a thing at all.
Maybe it's an ideal or a value,
The bright and shimmering city on the hill,
The utopic cradle of democracy,
The myth of the fifth morning or the Second Coming.
I think it's more about the seeking than the finding,
The journey, than the destination.
Something that makes the whole damn trip worth the effort.

Perhaps the sage advice of the masters,
The well-turned phrase of the pitch man,
The dirty martini at the end of a long day.
The sand mandalas of the Tibetan monks.
A family hand-me-down that means nothing to anyone but you.
A place you go so far down into yourself
That no one else could ever understand.
Maybe it's the Shaman's call,
The twenty-seven generations memorized
By African oral historians,
A flower pressed into a book someone gave you
Once in another life.
And maybe you just lead with your chin your whole life.

Maybe just the fact that you put your battered heart out there
Time and again
And took comfort in knowing that everyone's swan song ends up
Being what we collected, who we discarded, where we traveled,
And, most importantly, not the stuff we found along the way,
But what we did that added something to this world.

The editor didn't like my story about the wood carver
That's OK, their magazine, their style
But I felt bad about it
So I walked over to the carver's house to tell him
That's all right, he said, it isn't about notoriety
It's about art
But don't you want people to know about your craft, I asked
What I want, he said, is the weekend off for deer hunting

What I want is a new bird dog with the same smarts as old Sally
And for my daughter's boyfriend to not be such a jerk
For the bird feeder to fill itself for a change
I want fresh trout for breakfast every single morning
And for the moon to be full wherever I feel like it
Even so, I said, it would have been nice
To see someone have a little appreciation

You need to fight a few battles you can win, he said
You need more Zen and zeal
In your moon-of-the-misbegotten existence
Don't ask the branches to bend for your every whimsy
It doesn't really work that way
Try better carving tools and you still get a piece
That's only as good as your weakest hand
Your poorest eye and the grain of the wood
Hell, that's a whole other story

But this isn't just about disappointment, I said
It's an insult to the sensibilities
What the poet called "a little death"
Another chapter in the celestial tragi-comedy
I grow weary of a sun that rises every morning
On these indifferent soulless dwarves in giant's cloaks

Let's you and me can this crap, he said, let's go for a boat ride
We'll sidle up and down a few whitecaps
And talk about why white cedar's good as mahogany
Why you should always face west when you sleep
Why chicken doesn't taste good anymore
Why you cut down a tree with a whorl only on Thursdays
We're rich guys, you and me, he said
Who cares about fame and fortune

ELY, MINNESOTA

The crown jewel of the Arrowhead Region
In the Canadian Shield
On the Iron Range
By the berm of the Boundary Waters
On the verge of the Voyageur
Nestled near the the Superior National Forest
Ensconced by the International Border
Just below the Quetico, north of Palo and south of Nirvana
On the Echo Trail of the Heart
At the leeward ledge of the Laurentian Divide
Where the waters bend north to Hudson Bay
On a setback up the path from the North Shore
Just down stream from la Grand Portage
A stone's throw up the hill
From the world's greatest Freshwater Sea
On the first notch and buckle of the Volcanic Greenstone Belt

Perched on the oldest rock on this planet
2.7 billion years ancient
Where once the tallest mountains in the world
Higher than the Himalayas
Stretched their spires to the skies,
Where 12,000 years ago a glacial wall of ice a mile high
Rolled back to reveal the Land of 10,000 Lakes

The Lakes of Insula and Alice and White Iron and Shagawa
Of Vermilion and Burntside and This Man and That Man
Of Thumb and Finger and Pocket and Hula
The Lakes of Disappointment, Reflection, Confusion,
Superstition and Myth
Of Knife and Bow and Hatchet – of One and Two and Three

For this is a land where Ancients and Giants
And Legends once roamed
From Chief Hole In The Day and Bronco Nagurski
And Eric Sevareid
To Sigurd Olson and Dorothy Molter and Joe Seliga
Where for a thousand years
The Ojibwe defended their homelands
Defeating even the mighty Sioux and the Iroquois Confederacy
Where the bravest men who ever lived
Clambered down into the mines
To earn a living for their families

Where to this day you can drive down any road
And see a wolf, a bear, a moose, a cougar
Where the eagle soars above
And in the evening the great owls
Make their way to the rocky wood
Where beneath our canoes are fish larger than your children
And turtles older than your grandparents

Part fact, part fiction, fable and fish story: Ely, Minnesota
Tell the truth now. Is there any place you'd rather be
This day, this hour, this moment in history?
If so, then Godspeed on your journey.
As for the rest of us, we'll stay right here

At the far Eastern end of the Central Time Zone
In the Upper Midwest of the Lower 43
In the States which are United
On a continent so beautiful they named it after us –
'North' America –
On the third rock from the Sun which always shines
Even when there is too much snow to see it
And at night we're bathed in the light of the Aurora Borealis

was a cavalry cook,
In the Great War, The War To End All Wars,
The one before they knew enough to give them numbers.
And he rode high and dry in the cook wagon
As the doughboys slugged it out in the trenches of France.
All along that trail of tears
That years later in another war men would call
The Maginot Line
His friends died by the thousands.
My grandfather fed the rest
And sent them
Back to that glockenspiel
Of machine gun spray and mustard gas.

Years later
A retired diesel mechanic
He moved to northern Michigan
To gather the white-tail, the bluegill
And the bass.

He taught me how to drink whiskey
And how to read the Chicago Tribune
From cover to cover.
And how to sit out in a flannel shirt
In ninety-degree weather
And wave at the tourists
As they passed in their station wagons.

And once on an October midnight in 1957
He woke me and we walked together
To the edge of his property
And stood looking out
Across the waters of Hamlin Lake
At a shard of light
That moved in the sky
That he called a Sputnik.
"Isn't that something?" he said.

It was a new age.
One he knew he would not be a part of.
For he had seen the horse-drawn carts of death
And somehow machines moving through the night sky
Were not that impressive.
As we turned to go
He dropped down to one knee in the wet grass
And plucked a giant nightcrawler for the next day's bait.
Holding it up to the flashlight
He turned again to me and said,
"Now, isn't that something?"

A Small Incident of No Consequence

I pull up and the Canadian Border Guard asks me
What I do for a living. Now I know he's trained
To watch and listen to how I answer, not to care what I say.
I know you're trained to watch and listen to how I answer, I say.
A woman I dated worked in a Vet's psych hospital, I stammer,
It was the same deal. You sure? he asks,
And pushes some buttons on his computer.

And I used to work with emotionally impaired
And learning disabled teens too, I say,
But I can see I'm losing ground quickly.
You didn't answer the question, he says,
Shaking his head at the words appearing on his screen.
I'm in the show business, I finally admit.
Well, radio really, I qualify. What'd you do on the radio?
Recite poems from memory, play music,
Make up stuff to entertain people.
They pay you to do that, do they?

Sort of, I say. It's just part-time; I'm semi-retired.
Semi, huh? Any pepper spray, guns, alcohol, explosives or
Vegetables in the car?
Vegetables? I think to myself.
And for some reason I remember blowing up pumpkins
Using M-80s with my cousin Larry.
Not a one, I say with force and confidence. Nothing illegal.
I didn't say they were illegal, did I? he says.
And now it's me studying him for humor and body language.

But I can only see half of him over the partition
And the half I'm seeing is all business but getting bored.
Bringing anything else into Canada, he asks?
Just some of my money.
Limbaugh, he says. Are you on the radio like Rush Limbaugh?
And now I'm wondering what Rush is short for: Rushmore,
Rushmeister, Rushelstiltskin? No, I say. I'm not a conservative.
More a Doubting Thomas Moderate
With leanings to the left on Social Deconstruction Issues.

Spend much time in Canada, do you? he asks.
Not nearly enough, I say. I love Canada, except for the food.
No one ever says let's go out for Canadian tonight.
That's an old joke, he says, but I can see a hint of a smile
Under his reflector, aviator sunglasses. Rilke, he says.
Now there was a poet. And Rimbaugh and Rothke.
Hey, that rhymes.
I'm the poet now, aren't I? he says, with a real smile this time.
And then he waves and I drive into a foreign country.

BEAR

The Ancients say if you meet a bear in the woods
She will not look you in the eye; she'll look into your soul
To see if you should exist or not, a test few would welcome.
Whether *americanus* or *horribilis*, major or minor,
The Ursus bear and constellation vex and fascinate.
Even the word from which the Grizzly gets her name –
Horror – is an enigma.
In the Latinate it wasn't even a noun,
But a verb meaning the act of shaking.
And the animal herself is just as puzzling.

She's mostly a vegetarian who will eat any kind of meat.
She is slow and ponderous
But can outrun a horse in an open field
And anything alive going straight uphill.
Docile and shy,
She has the greatest muscle mass of all animals.
She even defies science by adding muscle
While sleeping for six months.
She is huge,
Yet by ratio gives birth to the smallest babies of any living thing.
She sleeps all winter
But her body temperature and metabolism hardly drop at all.
Proud and noble,
She will beg and dance and clown for a handout.
Her cholesterol is twice that of humans
Yet she doesn't get gallstones or heart problems.

WHEN I AM OLD

When I am old I shall wear a ball cap
From the St. Louis Browns
Because my grandfather once played in their farm system,
Or maybe a John B. Stetson hat, three-corner fold,
Four X and black chinos with both suspenders and a belt
And the knees ripped out, not as a fashion statement,
But from work.
And black biker boots and a T-shirt with the slogan
"I'm Working On My Issues."
I'll use a walking stick and not a cane
And have a key ring with about a hundred keys
And I won't know what any of them open and I won't care.

When I am old I'll drink whiskey in the morning
And coffee at night
And laugh and spit and swear wherever I want.
When I am old I'll help Girl Scouts across the street
Even if they don't want to go
And I won't have a car
And I won't have a bike
And I'll walk everywhere.

When I am old I'll have a dog named Sam Peckinpaw
And some summer's morning I'll lock up the house
And old Sam and I will walk over to see one of my sons
Even if he lives two states away.
When I am old I'll tell people exactly what I think of them
And surprisingly, most of the time it really will be good stuff.
When I am old I won't have a TV
And I won't have a radio
And I won't have a computer or a clock or a phone in the house.
I won't read books and I won't read magazines
And I won't read newspapers and maybe, finally
I'll learn something just watching the birds and the weather.

When I am old I'll build a tree house in the back yard
And stay in it for a month at a time.
I'll cut the grass with goats
And feed the neighbor's cat smoked fish in the back yard
And throw little stones at the starlings hogging the bird feeder
And I'll shoot off my shotgun on the important pagan holidays.
And all the kids on the block will ride by on their bikes
And yell at me that I'm as crazy as a loony bird
And they'll be right as rain.

And some October morning when I am very old,
I'll clear off the junk from the kitchen table
And sit down and write three short letters
To the people I loved most in this world
And then I'll walk out into the woods as far as I can get
And lie down under a big pine tree and stay there forever
And it will be as if I was never here at all.

Or maybe, just maybe,
I'll be walking along an old two-track road that morning
And God will tool up in a robin's egg blue '64 Ford Falcon.
And God will look just like Lucinda Williams
With a straw cowboy hat and boots
And she'll swing open the door and say, "Hop in cowboy."
And I'll get in and God will drive us back to her house
Way back in the woods next to some little trout stream
Which has no name.
And she'll pour us a couple of fingers of good blended whiskey
And go over to her Bang and Olafson hi-fi
And put on a few old vinyl records like John Lee Hooker
And Sam Bush and Ella Fitzgerald.
And we'll light up a couple of Pall Mall non-filters
And talk half the night about Modes Of Alienation In The
    Diminishing Diaspora Of Archetypal Representations Of
    Female Characteristics In Southern Gothic Literature
And the other half of the night we'll talk about fishing.

And somewhere 'long about dawn
I'll look over and see God stifling a yawn
And sneaking a peek at a watch
That has about a thousand time zones on it and I'll say
"It's OK, God, I know you've got stuff to take care of,
You run along now, I'll be just fine.
But I've got to say that, for the record,
You look pretty tough in those jeans, babe."

And God will come over and take me by the shoulders
And look me in the eye and kiss me on the nose and say,
"You know Ray,
You're not half as bad as everybody told me you were."

And I'll say, "You too God, you too!"

And God will drive away in that old Ford Falcon
With the rod knock and the bad muffler
And I'll turn around and be on that dock in front of a cottage
That doesn't even exist anymore except in my mind
And it will be the scene from a dream I had fifty years ago
And the circle will be complete.

And I'll turn around and look down the dock
And into the rising sun of some October morning
And that little kid who was me
Will walk out of the sunrise and take my own old hand
And I'll say to him:
"Let me show you a couple-a-things I learned about fishing."

And the whole story will start again.
Only maybe, just maybe this time, we'll get it all right.

Ray Nargis is an award-winning poet, short story, and non-fiction writer who grew up on a horse ranch near Ludington, Michigan, and spent the majority of his life teaching, working, and writing in northern Lower Michigan.

His work has appeared in newspapers, magazines, and anthologies including: *The World and I, The Red Cedar Review* (Prizewinner 1989), *The Garfield Review, The McGuffin Reader* (Prizewinner 1990), *The Detroit Free Press, Synapse Magazine, The Traverse City Record-Eagle,* and *The Glen Arbor Sun.*

Mr. Nargis received an undergraduate degree in journalism from Central Michigan University and a master's degree in creative writing from Michigan State University where he studied with the renowned poets Diane Wakoski and Robert Creeley.

In addition to teaching writing at Michigan State University, Northwestern Michigan College, and Bay Mills Community College, Mr. Nargis has served as a teacher and principal at both private and public high schools.

Ray Nargis apprenticed the craft of storytelling with the late Max Ellison during the last years of Ellison's life, and is a founding member of both the Stone Circle and Beach Bards Poetry groups. He has performed as an oral poet and storyteller for more than twenty-five years, including speaking at The National Storytelling Festival, Jonesbourgh, Tennessee and The National Governor's Conference in Traverse City, Michigan.

Mr. Nargis lives in Ely, Minnesota, and is the host of *The Pathways*, a popular Sunday morning radio program on local radio station, WELY, 94.5 FM.

He divides his time between fishing and paddling the rivers and lakes of northern Minnesota, a cabin in Ontario, and visiting his sons in San Francisco and Chicago.